The Lion Sti

Stories from Papua New Guinea and the Solomon Islands

Avonlea Woods Marvin

*For Earl, who enriches my life
by pushing me out of my comfort zone
and challenging me to embrace
life in a wider place.*

Contents

Introduction

"I just talked with John* in the World Mission department. Cross-cultural training for volunteers is being given this weekend. Applications are past due, but if we download the forms on the computer and hand-carry them to the office, maybe they'll accept us." My husband, Earl, was ecstatic with his good news.

"Why on earth would we want to do that?" I countered. We hadn't discussed this subject for a long time.

"Because we've always talked about volunteering overseas when we retired. This is our chance to do it."

That was certainly true, but now didn't seem to be a good time. We hadn't fully settled into our retirement home. For the first time, we were enjoying living near grandchildren. I didn't want to miss participation in their lives as we had done for years. My mind filled with the many reasons not to pursue this idea just now, but the *click-click-whirr* of the printer told me that, objections notwithstanding, we were applying to attend the seminar.

When Earl took our completed forms to the World Mission office he was handed a battery of tests for each of us to complete. There was a personality profile, a test to discover aptitudes for various jobs, and one to ascertain our abilities and adaptabilities to work in a cross-cultural setting.

Experienced missionaries who were expert communicators led the seminar. About thirty-five people attended, most of them single, but there were a few married couples. We were the senior members of the group.

We learned various concepts by role playing, problem solving, and confronting difficult circumstances we might encounter in cross-cultural situations. We learned to use alternative methods to achieve goals if the first two or three trials were unsuccessful. We laughed a lot. A few dropped out after the first day.

On the second day Earl and I were interviewed.

"Where do you want to go?"

"Anywhere we are needed," we replied.

"What would you like to do?"

Earl answered, "Anything we have the ability to do."

---

*Candidate coordinator

At that point I doubted that I had anything to offer.

"Sometimes it takes a year or more to match the field with the volunteer," David** explained.

I interpreted this warning as his polite way of saying, "Don't call us; we'll call you."

Less than a month later David called. "The missionaries in Papua New Guinea want you to come there," he said. "They need Earl for some maintenance projects at the mission station. Avonlea is needed in the field office. Does this sound like something you would be interested in?

I laughed aloud. I thought, *Papua New Guinea is not quite the last place I thought we would go—but only because it didn't cross my mind at all. Head hunters; tribesmen smeared with colored mud; rugged terrain; primitive living conditions; the world's last frontier.*

When Earl returned home I told him about the telephone call. He exclaimed, "Papua New Guinea! Of all places! That never crossed my mind." After fifty years of marriage we often express ourselves similarly.

"Papua New Guinea," we repeated at the same time and burst into laughter.

"They have tribal warfare there," I mused.

"Maybe not so much anymore," Earl said comfortingly.

"The men wear feathers on their heads and stick long, sharp things through their noses. They put mud on themselves and look very scary."

Earl didn't reply.

"Do they have snakes in New Guinea?" I pursued. I'd much rather face fierce warriors dressed and primed for battle than come across a snake in my path.

"I haven't heard snake stories from there like I've heard from Africa," he answered cautiously.

"There are no beauty salons in the highlands of New Guinea."

There was no way he could counter that argument. "Just stick a quill through your nose and daub yourself with clay and no one will notice your bad hair," Earl answered.

Ten months later we waved goodbye to friends and family and began the thirty-three-hour trip to Papua New Guinea.

**Volunteer coordinator

In our most confident, optimistic moments we could not have anticipated the joy, inspiration, friendships, adventures, and spiritual growth we would experience during the next six months. Our lives were enriched by association with missionaries, other volunteers, and national Christians. Our preconceived ideas were challenged every day and drove us to study the culture, the Bible, and our own hearts more deeply than we had ever done. During our time in PNG, I wondered how much my Christianity is influenced by Western customs and religious tradition and how much is due to the atoning blood of Christ. I learned to withhold judgment when people acted within the bounds of their own culture instead of according to my ideas of right and wrong.

Missionaries work diligently to teach PNG Christians how to honor Christ in their families and tribal relationships. PNG Christian leaders are showing the Way to others, and the seed is bearing fruit.

1. The Lion Still Roars
Mike Ward's Story*

"Be alert and of sober mind. Your enemy the devil prowls around like a roaring lion looking for someone to devour. Resist him, standing firm in the faith, because you know that the family of believers throughout the world is undergoing the same kind of sufferings."
—1 Peter 5:8–9

"Do you know who I am?" the man asked. "I am Satan, and I am full of hatred. I am going to kill you."

In September 2004, when I was seventeen, my father asked me to go to the Solomon Islands to film the highlights of the work of the *Jesus Film* teams. It didn't take much to convince me to go. My family had visited there five years before, and I had been hoping for an opportunity to go back.

I felt inadequate for the task ahead of me, though. As I boarded the plane to fly to Honiara, the capital of the Solomons, I remembered Dr. Bill McCoy's story of being greatly discouraged during his first term of missionary service. He was ready to return home because he felt he could not meet the requirements for a missionary doctor. But God came to him and said, *"You're right. You are inadequate for this task. You don't have what it takes, but I do."* With these words ringing in my ears, I knew I could do anything God wanted me to do.

I spent the weekend in the home of missionaries George and Nancy Miller. George asked me to speak to the youth group after church on Sunday, and I gladly accepted. God came and helped me in that service. I spoke about how abundantly he blesses and takes care of us when we put our trust in him and have faith that he will provide whatever we need.

---

*This chapter is written from Mike's perspective, as told to the author of this book. Mike Ward grew up in Papua New Guinea, where his parents, Verne and Natalie, were missionaries for many years. As of this book's writing (2008), Mike was living in Nampa, Idaho.

The next day George, eight members of a *Jesus Film* team, and I traveled to Mage (pronounced MAH-gee), the small village where I would document on film the work of the church and its beginnings. Pastor Edmund took us to his house, where we would be staying with some of his family members.

Our days started at five o'clock in the morning, and we spent each day interviewing people and videotaping scenes for our project. We recreated and filmed key events in the life of the church.

Every evening we showed the *Jesus Film*, *The Passion of the Christ*, or *Hellfire*, a movie made in the seventies. Most, if not all, of the village people attended each night. After every showing we gave an invitation, and each time several people came forward to surrender their lives to Christ.

God was doing miracle work in Mage. Sinners were forgiven; hearts were made pure. The animist religion was being replaced by the gospel of Christ. I was surprised to hear some of the nationals saying, "I can't believe we're not getting more opposition."

"What kind of opposition?" I asked.

"From the evil spirits," they replied. "They can't be happy."

They began to tell of the many evil spirits who roamed the area. One spirit reportedly took the form of an elderly woman who possessed extraordinary strength. It was said she had thrown one man against a tree. I listened skeptically. It all sounded to me like some of the ghost stories I had heard around campfires.

One Saturday night we organized a prayer chain to pray for God's blessing on the Sunday service and on the film that would be shown the next evening. From nine o'clock that night until six o'clock Sunday morning different groups came to the church every hour to pray for sixty minutes. Not wanting to miss anything, I spent the entire night filming and praying with them. I fell into bed at six o'clock on Sunday morning and slept until eight.

The church service began at ten o'clock, and the preaching ended at noon. However, no one wanted to leave. People stood up, one after the other, to give testimony or to sing a special song. God moved the hearts of everyone there. Finally, at half past two, we had to end the service because we had promised to show the *Jesus Film* that evening in another village far up in the mountains.

It was dusk when we arrived in Aura, where we were to show the film. The people who had invited us gave a warm welcome to their home, but I could not rid myself of the feeling of darkness I had experienced when we entered the village.

We began to set up our equipment. As I worked, I saw a bright light fly across the sky. It resembled a ball of fire. Traveling at a great rate of speed, it dipped to pass just over us and disappeared into the valley.

"Did you see that?" I asked a villager.

"Oh, yeah. We see those a lot around here."

"What was it?"

"It was an evil spirit sent to kill someone—probably the father of this house."

I was surprised at how calmly he shrugged and accepted this as a common occurrence. He continued, "A witch doctor lives on top of that mountain. He uses that   spirit to kill people. It will come and attack someone, even in the middle of a group of people, and that person will fall dead. And did no one tell you that two people from this family have died in the last two months? It is said that evil spirits killed them."

I could hardly believe it. To make sure I wasn't imagining everything, I asked other team members if they had seen the bright light. They had. The thought occurred to me that maybe the ball of fire had been sent for someone on our team and that, for some reason, the attack had been aborted.

The villager told me that on more than one occasion he had seen two lights of different colors speed across the sky and collide, sending down "a rain of stars." These lights, he said, were evil spirits.

I had never been in a place thought to be haunted by demons. I continued to feel a power of darkness, although I didn't know what to think or believe about the events and conversation of the last few minutes.

We showed the *Jesus Film* that night, and to everyone's delight the father of the household repented and asked Christ into his heart.

All during the film I felt God talking to me. *"Are you ready to do anything for me?"* he asked.

I told him that was the reason I had come to the Solomon Islands.

"Are you ready to have complete faith in me?" he probed.

I spent the entire evening asking God to prepare me for whatever was to come.

"Are you ready to take on spiritual warfare?" God persisted.

I asked him to open my eyes to the evil around me and to fill me with his holy presence.

"Give me wisdom and strength to face whatever is coming," I petitioned.

Deep in my spirit God clearly told me to prepare to face the forces of evil.

"I'm happy to do what you want," I prayed. "But I'm so inadequate, Lord." Immediately I was filled with peace.

When our equipment was packed in the truck, more people wanted to ride back to Mage than had ridden to Aura. There was not room for everyone in the truck, so a few of us decided to walk.

We came down the mountain to the main road, which could have been traveled only on foot or by a four-wheel-drive vehicle. I could still feel pervasive darkness and evil. I knew, without hearing anything or looking back, that a man was following us. I also knew exactly how close he was to us. I turned around and beamed my flashlight directly on him. He was still about sixty yards away.

He ran toward us, yelling that he was the devil. "Turn that light off, or I'll kill you!" he shouted.

I obeyed him, but two of us stepped directly into his path.

He came within twenty yards of us, and we could hear him muttering in what seemed to be a tribal language.

Soon he was walking directly behind us, speaking in a loud, angry voice. However, before long he stepped away from us. We quickly walked ahead of him to get to the safety of the village.

The man followed us the few miles back to Mage. When we got there God seemed to say to me, *"Wait here. I want you to talk to this guy."*

My companions continued into the village.

The man began walking faster. Catching up to me, he grabbed the front of my shirt and put his face near mine. "Do you know who I am?" he asked. "I'm the devil, and I'm going to kill you here tonight."

Unlike other Solomon Islanders, who speak Pidgin English, this man spoke perfect American English without any trace of an island accent.

I looked at him and said, "No, you're not going to kill me—because I have Christ in me to protect me."

He took my hand and led me over to a log, where he had me sit beside him. "I am Satan, and I will kill everyone here on earth. Only a few will be spared because they are my people. Everyone else will be killed."

"I am so sorry that you have so much hatred in you," I replied.

"I am Satan, and I am full of hatred. You, you are going to die here tonight. I am going to kill you, and the police can't stop me."

The peace I had felt earlier enveloped me in this moment. It was as though I was outside myself, observing the scene from a distance.

"I do not need protection from the police because I have Christ in me," I said. "If you kill me, it will be only because God has allowed it. I don't believe he will permit you to do that."

The man rose from the log and stepped aside. He seemed to be thinking about what to do next. He came back.

"What do you want from me? I will give you anything you want. Do you want sexual powers? You play the guitar." (How did he know that?) "I'll give you music talent. Do you want to be a sports star? Power, talent, money? I can give you whatever you want."

I answered, "I do not need anything from you. I have Jesus Christ, and that is all I need."

The man countered, "The Bible says that a ruler will be raised up from the east. I am that ruler. I am neither white nor black. I am both, and I will be king over both white and black. I will kill you; then I will kill Jesus."

With authority I didn't know I had, I said to him, "You will fail in killing me, and you will fail in killing Jesus. You will be defeated."

The man did not reply; instead, he walked away. I stayed seated, trying to understand what had taken place. I thought this must have been an insane man who was hallucinating.

But I felt God saying, *"No, he is not a lunatic."*

I returned to the house, feeling no fear. Indeed, the overpowering sense of peace and calm, beyond my ability to understand, continued to be present.

It had been a long day, and the team members were exhausted. I was sharing a bedroom with George and one of the pastors who was working with us. "You didn't come back tonight when the others did. What were you doing?" George asked.

I told him about my encounter. He was surprised by my account and gently probed to determine whether I had imagined this fantastic story.

George, a man in his forties, had served as missionary in Papua New Guinea for several years and in the Solomon Islands for the past five years. He knew that spiritual warfare is overtly waged in both places, although he had not personally been involved in this form of it. He became convinced that my experience was real.

We continued to talk about how we had seen God in action all weekend. We spoke of how many had been saved and the transformations that had taken place.

Suddenly, as if to confirm my story, a loud noise came from outside. It sounded as though someone had slammed two pieces of hard wood together. We heard it again, and then it was repeated on the front steps of the house. George and I both felt an intense darkness. A heavy pressure crushed my chest. I couldn't speak.

George quickly sat up in his bed and said, "In the name of Jesus Christ, I command whatever is here to leave."

No sooner had the words left his mouth than we heard what sounded like a large group of people running down the hall. The house shook as though in an earthquake. The door to our room was closed, but the air seemed to be sucked out the window. Fresh air blew in.

We sat in stunned silence for a minute, and I said, "Uncle George, I think you scared something off."

Strangely, the pastor who was in the same room with us remained serenely asleep. I felt we should check on the men who were sleeping in the living room near the front door. I directed a flashlight beam toward one of them, Richard. For the first time George and I felt fear.

Richard lay with his head thrown back in an unnatural position. His eyes were half open and glazed over. We couldn't see his chest moving. After we observing him for what seemed to be a long time, he finally took a breath and his appearance returned to normal.

"You know, George," I said. "There is a spiritual battle going on out there right now, and I think we are just on the brink of it."

I had no idea how truly I spoke.

Outside, the dog began to whine and then began running. Looking out the window, George and I couldn't see anything, but we could hear the spirits moving around outside the house.

They came up the steps to the door, and the door shook. We walked through the house, praying in each room and at every window in the house. We prayed for the safety of the team members, some sleeping in two other houses. Our prayers were uttered in a normal tone of voice. No one else awoke. The two men in the living room had not stirred when I first flashed the light on them.

Throughout the rest of the night, George and I maintained a prayer vigil. When we heard something on the steps, one of us rebuked it in Jesus's name, and the noise went away. We heard rattling and shaking in other parts of the house. With Christ's authority we took turns demanding that whatever was threatening us leave. It always obeyed.

About 3:30 in the morning, we heard a strange sound coming from the woods around us. I can best describe it as someone with a bad sense of rhythm striking a tree with an axe. When it began, it sounded distant, but it kept getting closer and closer until it seemed the sound was coming from under the house. The presence of evil was palpable. Both George and I quickly rebuked it and in Jesus's name commanded it to leave. We heard it once more, this time far distant from us. It had fled.

It must have been 4:30 when I felt directed to pray aloud and set a spiritual boundary around Mage. Christ's presence came into me and gave me the authority to do so. Going to the open window, I said to the spirits, "You have no authority here. This is God's land, and these are his people. In the name of Jesus Christ, my Lord and Savior, I command all evil to flee from this place. You are no longer welcome here. You know your boundaries. You know that this land was given to the Lord. It is covered by the blood of Christ. You are no longer allowed to roam in it." I mentioned several landmarks around the village. "They will be covered by his blood. I claim this village for him."

Then George and I prayed for the Lord to surround us with his angels and to protect Mage from the evil that harassed it. At that time we both felt released from the burden of prayer.

We slept soundly from five until six o'clock.

While we ate breakfast, we told the other team members about the events of the night.

To my surprise, none of them had heard anything. Jimmy said, "I did wake up for a minute last night, but I couldn't get up. It was as though I was overcome with exhaustion. It seemed that something was keeping me from raising up."

Later I found that Satan had attacked other people. Willie had been out on his daily jog on Saturday. An old woman ran out of the bushes and chased him. He knew it to be the evil spirit who was often seen around Mage. Even though she looked to be very old, Willie started running at top speed to get away from her. She caught up with him and grabbed him. He is a muscular soccer player, but the woman threw him against a tree and ran away.

Willie was a Solomon Islander in his twenties. He had been a Christian for only four or five months when this satanic siege began. On Sunday, while the team went to Aura to show the film, he had stayed at the house to act as guard. Hearing the dog whine, he opened the door to see what was bothering it. The animal burst into the house. He was not allowed to be in the house, and Willie shoved him back outside. The dog pushed his way in again. This unusual behavior prompted Willie to look around and see what had frightened the dog.

He saw that the yard surrounding the house was full of people. As Willie looked at them, their appearances changed, and he realized they were evil spirits. When they began to advance toward the house, Willie began to pray. He had no sooner said, "Jesus Christ" than, as Willie related to us, "They ran into the jungle. There were tons of them. It was like water flowing into the trees."

Comparing times of day, we realized this had happened around the same time that God was impressing upon me that I would be called upon to do spiritual warfare.

The whole team thanked the Lord for his protection and guidance. We realized that God's amazing work that weekend had threatened Satan and his kingdom. We knew that we were helpless in our own strength but that God had given victory over the devil and his demons.

Jesus once sent seventy-two ambassadors to prepare the way for him to enter villages and towns throughout Judea. They "returned [to Jesus] with joy and said, 'Lord, even the demons submit to us in your name.' He replied, 'I saw Satan fall like lightning from heaven. I have given you authority to trample on snakes and scorpions and to overcome all the power of the enemy; nothing will harm you. However, do not rejoice that the spirits submit to you, but rejoice that your names are written in heaven'" (Luke 10:17–20).

Before this experience, I did not understand how real the spirit world is. I thank God for challenging my faith and helping me grow spiritually through this encounter with Satan and his demons. I am humbly grateful, too, that he has forgiven my sins and written my name in the Lamb's Book of Life.

Mike Ward

2. The Lion's Teeth Are Broken

"At the breath of God . . . the teeth of the great lions are broken."
—Job 4:9a, 10b
"In your anger do not sin . . . and do not give the devil a foothold."
—Ephesians 4:26a, 27

"I will not let Satan have the last word in this matter." Sarah's eyes flashed, and her mouth pressed into a grim thin line as she rose from her knees. "I will tell Nua about Jesus and take her to church with me. I will keep on working for God, no matter what Wusik does." The determination that God planted in Sarah that day would carry her through a lifetime of service to her Lord.

Sarah was different from her PNG friends. Even though she could neither read nor write, she possessed remarkable intelligence. In a society that places small value on women, Sarah became a spiritual leader, respected by both nationals and missionaries.

To help me understand her own story, Sarah first told me about Wusik, a story that began in the early 1940s.

"When Wusik was a young man, there was a big war in New Guinea. The Japanese tried to take the island for themselves, and the white people fought back. The soldiers in the Australian army got him to work in their camp. He carried water, cooked meals, washed and pressed their uniforms, and kept their *haus* clean. They taught him to speak Pidgin English. He learned the ways of white men. When the fighting was over, he came back to our village, and we were married. My name at that time was Kini. We have three *pikinini meri*" (daughters).

One evening in 1954, as Wusik and the other men in his village huddled around the fire, one of them had astonishing news.

"Waitpela i kam long Kudjip." (A white man has come to Kudjip.) He had everyone's attention. Kudjip was not far from their village of Kawi.

"Bilong wanem em kam?" (Why did he come?)

"Mi no save." (I don't know.)

Wusik listened as the others discussed the possible reasons for the white man's presence and what it might mean for the villagers. An idea began to form. Since Wusik spoke fluent Pidgin

English and was familiar with the ways of white men, he might be able to work for the newcomer and earn some *kina* shells.

The next day Wusik dressed in his best attire. Bare to the waist, a knee-length string apron in the front and a leafy branch covering his hips, he walked barefoot up the muddy trail to Kudjip.

The village of Kudjip was situated on land between two warring tribes. The Australian government had given the land between the tribes to the Church of the Nazarene. Officials hoped the gospel of Christ would bring some stability, and maybe peace, to the volatile area.

"Apinun!" (Good afternoon.) Wusik greeted the smiling white man.

"Apinun!" missionary Sidney Knox returned his greeting.

"Nem bilong mi Wusik," Wusik introduced himself. *"Nem bilong yu?"*

Sidney was puzzled.

"Wusik," the highlander repeated, pointing to himself.

Sidney hoped he understood. "Sidney," he replied, hand on his chest.

"Yu tok Pisin?" (Do you speak Pidgin English?)

"Nogat," Sidney answered. *"Yu lainim mi?"* (No. Will you teach me")

Before Wusik returned to Kawi, he had agreed to come back to Kudjip to teach Pidgin English to Wanda and Sidney Knox, the missionaries sent by the Church of the Nazarene to the Papua New Guinea Highlands.

After a few days of language instruction, Sidney was able to tell Wusik that he had come to the Highlands to bring the good news about *Bikpela* (God) and his *pikinini* (son), Jesus.

Back at Kawi, Wusik answered the question, "Why did he come?"

"Waitman tok gutpela tok long Papa God na pickinini man bilong God, nem Jesus." (The white man speaks good words about Father God and his Son, Jesus.) He told them about Sidney and the amazing *kago* he had brought to the Highlands. He said he would return to Kudjip to teach the missionary and his wife how to speak Pidgin English.

Sidney soon realized that Wusik was not a typical PNG Highlander. His teaching ability became apparent as Sidney and

Wanda struggled with Pidgin English, the trade language established so government officials and the hundreds of language groups in PNG could communicate with each other. Government officials often called Wusik to Mt. Hagan, the Western Highlands Province capital, to translate between Pidgin English and a tribal language.

"Mi helpim mek ples," volunteered Wusik, surveying the *kago* the Knoxes had brought from America.

Sidney's quizzical look told Wusik that the white man had not understood his friendly offer.

After a few more lessons, Sidney learned that Wusik's proposal was an offer to help him build his house. Wusik was astonished when he helped unload the parts for a prefabricated house from a shipping container at the site of the developing mission station.

He and Sidney learned together as they erected the *kapa* (metal) house. While they worked, Sidney told him about *Bikpela* and his *pikinini man,* Jesus.

Since Wusik was working long hours on the mission station, he built his own hut on the grounds and began staying days and nights. But he missed Kini. He decided to bring her to meet his new friends.

As well as he could, he explained their strange ways, even though he himself didn't understand all of them. "The missionary has a *kapa haus na planti kago* (metal house and many possessions). You will like the white *meri nem* Wanda. Come on. Go with me," he coaxed.

Nothing he said convinced Kini. White people were different from Highlands people. She had heard whispered stories about the white men who had come twenty years before. She was afraid of them and refused to go.

Wusik had a winning argument. "If you go, they will teach you about Papa God." This interested Kini. For several months some unnamed hunger had sent her to the only church in her village. The service was conducted in Latin, and she didn't understand what the *Bikpela* (big or important man) in the front of the church was saying, or the rituals of the *Misa* (Mass). When she questioned Wusik, he said he didn't understand either.

"We could only watch the ritual," Sarah said later. "We couldn't take part in the service. No one taught us about God, Jesus, sin, the Bible, prayer, or anything about being a Christian." Kini was willing to risk going to Kudjip if the missionaries would teach her about God.

Wanda was kind to Kini and won her acceptance. But in spite of the missionaries' invitations and Wusik's urging, Kini refused to attend church. She did not know how to conduct herself during the service. She didn't think it proper to attend church in PNG fashion—bare to the waist, thighs exposed, with only an ankle-length skirt covering her abdomen and hips. Wusik continued to urge Kini to gospel.

One Sunday morning Kini decided to accompany Wusik. She made history by being the first Highlands woman to attend a Nazarene church service. Wanda and Sidney sang songs that sounded strange to Kini's ears. After they had sung for a while, Sidney raised his hands palms upward, signifying that the congregation was to stand for prayer.

"When I stood for prayer, an evil spirit attacked me," Sarah said. "I fainted and fell to the floor."

Wanda and Sidney immediately knelt beside her and began to pray for her. In a few minutes Kini regained consciousness, and Sidney continued the service. Even though she did not accept Christ at that time, Kini knew that the evil spirit was gone and would not bother her again.

Wutsik continued his work on the mission station. When Sidney started a school for boys, some of them were boarding students. Wusik washed their clothing and cooked for them.

Kini became Wanda's *haus meri* (house woman). Wanda was learning to cook and care for her family without any of the conveniences, including electricity, that she'd had in the United States. All her time was taken with even the simplest chores of daily living. By teaching Kini to help her, she could eventually be free to do the ministry she was called to do.

"I had a lot to learn," Sarah said, smiling. "I didn't know anything about white people's houses or keeping them clean. I didn't know what soap was. I didn't know how to cook white people's food. I had always cooked over an open fire and had never used salt. Wanda taught me how to use soap to wash dishes, clothes, and myself. I was afraid of the propane cooking stove, but Wanda encouraged me, and I learned."

Kini began to entertain thoughts of wearing western clothes. Her native garb gave little protection from the cold Highland nights and mornings. Wanda was more than willing to give clothing to her *haus meri* for both warmth and modesty's sake.

"At first I couldn't figure out how to wear them." Sarah laughed at the memory. "I tried to wear the clothes Wanda gave to me with my native dress. So sometimes I would wear my string skirt over the clothes she gave to me, and sometimes underneath. I didn't know there was a difference between front and back. Sometimes I wore underthings properly, and sometimes I wore them on the outside. I didn't know there was an inside and outside to the clothes. I know now that Wanda probably was amused at the spectacle I made."

Sidney had been struggling with explaining Christian baptism to his congregation. He especially needed help explaining the concept of immersion. Sidney persuaded Wusik and Kini to help him demonstrate that mode of baptism to the others. The next Sunday, Sidney led the crowd to the river that flowed through the valley near the church. After explaining again about being buried with Christ in baptism, Sidney plunged first Wusik and then Kini into the water. The others were relieved when Sidney brought them out of the water unharmed. This live object lesson taught them the mechanics of immersion, even though they were still learning the meaning of baptism.

After months of hearing the gospel and asking questions, both Kini and Wusik repented of their sins and asked Christ to live inside them. Then they were truly baptized and joined the church, Kini being the first PNG woman to do so. At that time she took the name Sarah, which means "princess."

Sarah became a dedicated Bible student, eager to learn everything about being a follower of Christ. Wanda invited Sarah to accompany her to the surrounding villages, where she taught the women and children about God. Since they could not read or write, the missionary taught by using large charts on which stick figures illustrated the Bible stories and Scripture verses. Soon Sarah was telling the stories and helping villagers memorize Scripture passages. She had a gift for applying Christian concepts to PNG culture. Eventually Wanda multiplied her own ministry by sending Sarah to one village while she went to another.

One Sunday Sarah decided to take her stick-figure chart and preach in a nearby village. Her ministry was successful, and soon she was going alone, taking the gospel to more and more villages.

Sarah wanted to teach her people Christian songs, but Western music was incomprehensible to them. Undaunted, she taught Christian words for the tunes they already knew. To this day those songs are sung in the bush churches every Sunday.

Sidney was impressed with Wusik's and Sarah's spiritual growth and the gift for ministry God had given them. Sidney talked with Wusik about the future. "You and Sarah are learning a lot about Jesus, and both of you have a talent for teaching and leading others. I would like to send you to Bible school, where you can learn more about God. At the Bible school you can learn to serve God even more effectively, maybe as a pastor. Sarah would be a great influence among the women. Would both of you pray about it? If this is God's will for you, he will let you know."

One morning, before Wusik started his work at the boys' school, he approached Sidney. "Missionary, Sarah and I have prayed and asked God if we should go to Bible school. We believe he wants us to go." Wanda and Sidney were overjoyed that Sarah and Wusik would prepare for Christian service. Taking their three little girls with them, they left Kudjip to attend Bible school.

Wusik and Sarah were happy. While Wusik learned theology, church administration, and leadership concepts, Sarah learned about being the wife of a Christian leader. Inside and outside the classroom, godly instructors modeled servant leadership and humble obedience to God. The concepts they learned challenged them. They were eager to learn all they could and put it into practice. But Satan stood in the wings, watching and planning.

One day Wusik's brother appeared on the Bible school campus. "You and I own a large area of tribal land," he reminded Wusik. "But we are in danger of losing it because we have no sons. You have three daughters and no sons. I have married several wives but have no children at all. I can't afford to buy any more wives, and you have only one. It's up to you to take another wife, who will give you *pikinini man.*

Wusik agreed that the family would lose their land if there were no sons to inherit it. Such a possibility was unthinkable. Wusik swallowed hard at his predicament. He had learned that God said when two people marry they are one flesh and the bond should not be broken. He knew that plural wives were not a part of his newfound faith in God. But he dared not lose the land that belonged to him and his brother. He could see no way but to do as his brother and his culture dictated that he do; he would have to take another wife.

Sarah reminded him that plural marriage could not be reconciled with the things they had learned about following Christ. Missionaries at the Bible school counseled with him. When their pleas went unheeded, they reminded Wusik that taking another wife would disqualify him for Christian leadership and education at the Bible school.

The pull of the culture was stronger than any other force, however. Wusik returned to Kawi, where he took a young girl, Nua, as his second wife. Sarah and the children returned to the mission station.

When New Guineans become angry, they do not consider themselves hot-*headed*. Their emotions originate in their *bels* (bellies), and they become hot in their bellies. "When I came back from the Bible school I was *belhat*. I felt bad toward Wusik. I tried to argue and fight with him. I still felt God's call to Christian work. I didn't think I could continue if Wusik was not involved."

"Why are you keeping me from God's work?" Sarah demanded of Wusik.

"Don't talk back to me," Wusik shouted. In keeping with PNG culture, Sarah received a beating for talking back to him.

Sarah was despondent. Her work for the Lord was finished. Sidney and Wanda, along with the other missionaries, felt crushed with disappointment. They had counted on Wusik to be a leader in bringing the gospel to his fellow Highlanders and to far-flung areas of the island.

When Sarah resumed her duties as the Knoxes' *haus meri,* Wanda encouraged her that God still had a place for her in his service, even if Wusik no longer qualified for Christian leadership. To Sarah's surprise, Wusik encouraged her to continue her work for God. She resumed teaching in the villages. She accompanied the missionaries to other places on the island to conduct evangelistic meetings.

In the absence of roads across the country, travel was by airplane. On the ground the bird-like contraption looked much larger and more intimidating than the ones she had seen flying high in the sky. Sarah smiled as she remembered how she and her friends had fled into the bush when they first saw an airplane flying across the sky. They thought it was an evil spirit and escaped to the bush so its shadow could not fall on them and bring calamity to them. How thankful she is that God delivered her from the power of evil spirits. Knowing that missionaries often flew, and always ready for adventure, Sarah boarded the plane with only slight misgivings. She became the first Western Highlands woman to fly.

After Sarah stayed at the mission station for five months, the missionaries encouraged her to return to Wusik. They counseled her to not argue with him about his new wife but to live Jesus in their presence every day. They promised their concern and prayers for her and her new circumstances.

At this point that Sarah declared that Satan would not gain victory in her situation. "I humbled myself before the Lord and went back to Wusik," she said. When she and the children entered their little grass home in Kawi, she explained her return. "Wusik, we both know God's Word about this matter. But you took Nua as your wife anyway. I will not fight with you or Nua. I will look after Nua. I will take her to church with me."

Wusik recognized that only God could give Sarah this attitude of acceptance. In every plural marriage Wusik knew there were jealousy, bitterness, and violence between the wives. Sometimes one wife solved the problem by murdering the other. He was relieved that Sarah's attitude reflected the love of Christ.

Sarah and Nua had known each other as children. Nua's father was the head man in his village. He was not a Christian; indeed, he knew nothing of Christ. When he asked Nua if she would like to marry Wusik, she had said, "No. He already has a wife." Nua did not want to live with the wrath of a first wife.

"He wants to marry you," Nua's father had replied. "He is wealthy. He has lots of land. If you don't take him, what will you do? Where will you go?" At best, unmarried women are considered to be only half the worth of a married one; at worst, she is thought of as a liability to the tribe. Other young women in her village were envious of her opportunity to marry a prosperous man who would probably become head man in his village.

Sarah and one of the missionaries visited her. They tried to dissuade her from marrying Wusik by reasoning with her and reading passages from the Bible concerning God's standards for marriage. This did not impress Nua; she knew nothing of the Christian God or his book.

She actually had no control over whom she married. Sometimes fathers refused to accept a bride price from someone his daughter did not want to marry, but the father always had final authority.

The contrast between the two wives was evident. Sarah was deeply committed to Christ; Nua knew nothing about him. Sarah was tall and had large bones; Nua was short and looked frail. Sarah was forthright and had opinions of her own; Nua was shy and quiet. Both possessed a sense of humor. Sarah's bright eyes sparkled, and a broad smile lit her face. Nua's eyes twinkled, and her little smile seemed to say, *I know something you don't know.*

By the time Sarah returned to Wusik, Nua was expecting their first child. It was a difficult pregnancy, and Sarah began taking care of her. She expressed concern and tenderness toward Nua and told her about Jesus's love. Before long Sarah realized that the baby had died. She knew Nua needed more help than could be given her in the village.

After kneeling beside Nua and praying for her, Sarah walked to Kudjip to get help from the missionaries. The first one she met was Wallace White. "Nua's baby has died," she said. "We must get help for her."

At that time there was no hospital on the mission station. They would have to take Nua to the government hospital for treatment. Driving over rough bush trails, through streams, and across land belonging to possibly hostile tribes, Sarah and Wallace took Nua ten miles to the hospital.

Nua was frightened. She had known women to die in childbirth. She had feelings of guilt about marrying Wusik. Maybe God was punishing her for marrying him. But Sarah's presence comforted her. She knew Sarah was praying to her God on her behalf.

The baby boy Wusik had desired was stillborn, delivered by Cesarean section. As Nua struggled to wake from the anesthetic, she became conscious that Sarah and Wallace were standing beside her, praying for her.

The next day when Nua was fully awake, Sarah and Wallace explained to her how to become a child of Sarah's God. Sarah's teachings made sense to Nua, and she repented of her sins and accepted Christ. As PNG custom dictates, Sarah stayed with Nua in the hospital, providing basic nursing care until Nua was discharged.

Nua eventually had four children, two girls and two boys. Her pregnancies were always difficult, and Sarah helped her through each one. She took responsibility for two families, two gardens, her pigs and Nua's pigs, and cooking food that would strengthen Nua and her unborn children. When the time came, she delivered the babies herself.

In spite of Nua's best efforts, she could not produce as many sons as Wusik wished. He took a third wife, who died when she delivered her first baby. Sarah took the little boy and raised him as her own.

It was apparent that Wusik had married Nua only to get sons. He did not give her the help PNG men usually give their wives. Nua, small in stature and frail, did the work of a man. She spaded her own garden and dug trenches around it to drain off water from the tropical rains. She cut trees for firewood. She wanted her sons to get an education, so she raised coffee beans, which she sold to pay school fees. In all this, Sarah helped Nua in addition to caring for her own responsibilities. She and Nua came to love each other as sisters.

"Sarah has always been good to me," Nua said. If she picked a flower for herself, she picked one for me. If she cooked a chicken, she gave me half. If she bought food at the market, she gave half to me. Today I am with Sarah's Lord. She showed me to follow Christ. We are together in this way."

The years sped on. Sarah and Nua never stopped praying for Wusik. After several years he came back to the Lord. He is in church with his wives every Sunday, but because he has plural wives, he cannot hold an office in the church. His natural leadership abilities and wealth have made him head man in his village. His wisdom and influence make him a respected member of the board at the Nazarene hospital in Kudjip.

God honored Sarah's humble spirit by giving success to her children. A job in an oil company brought prosperity to one daughter.

She built a *kapa* home for herself and her parents in Kawi. Another daughter's husband is the PNG ambassador to Belgium. When Sarah visited her, the daughter took Sarah to Russia. Nua's oldest daughter is Meti, whose story is told in the next chapter.

Not long ago, Sarah and Nua attended a Nazarene district women's meeting, where the problems of living for Christ in a plural marriage were addressed. The speaker, a woman national, was forceful in her condemnation of men taking multiple wives and of women allowing themselves to become plural wives. When she concluded her speech, the large group was divided into two smaller groups for mutual support and prayer. Since their problems are different, one group was for first wives, the other for second and third wives. The testimonies Nua heard from other women in similar situations convinced her that she needed to take one more step.

During the church service the next Sunday morning, shy little Nua stood. She had never spoken publicly, but she was obeying the Lord. She knew he would help her.

"I was thinking," she began, "that I should say sorry to Sarah and Wusik. I spoiled their marriage. I didn't want to marry him; I was forced to do it. I am sorry. Sarah is not my enemy. She is my first sister. I am her second sister. We are together in serving God."

She turned to Sarah, who was seated nearby. "I want to go to heaven. I believe in God. He has forgiven me. I want you to forgive me." There were few dry eyes in the congregation as Nua went to Sarah and the two women embraced. Sarah assured Nua that she was forgiven.

Nua then addressed the parents of young women. "Parents, don't give your daughters as plural wives, no matter how big the bride price the man offers or how rich he is." She turned to the girls, who now enjoy more freedom of choice than she had when she was young. "Girls, even if a man promises you a lot of pretty clothes and chicken to eat every day, don't become a second or third wife. It is not pleasing to God. As a second wife, I can be only a half church member," Nua explained. This means that she could never hold office or teach a Sunday school class. "But I want to work for God. So I clean the church and put flowers around the front. Sarah and I can join hands and together work for God until we die."

Age and hard work have brought physical decline to Sarah. She is almost blind. The strong body that once did the work of two women and one man tires easily now.

"Sarah helped me for a long time," said Nua with a bright smile. "Now I can help Sarah. I work her garden, tend her pigs, and help her in her *haus.*"

Sarah and Nua came together to be interviewed, and their affection for each other was evident. I asked them if I could write their story and tell it to others when I returned to the United States. They were happy to give permission. Sarah said, "There was another lady who humbled herself before God, and her story was told all over the world. Her name was Esther."

3. The Lion's Mouth Is Shut

"At my first defense, no one came to my support, but everyone deserted me. May it not be held against them. But the Lord stood at my side and gave me strength, so that through me the message might be fully proclaimed and all the Gentiles might hear it. And I was delivered from the lion's mouth."
—*2 Timothy 4:16–17*

"One of these men wants you for his wife," Wusik told his sixteen-year-old daughter, Meti. "He has paid a big bride price for you. He and some other men from his village have come to take you to his home."

Meti looked at the men and didn't recognize any of them. Her papa did not point out the man he had chosen for her, nor did he introduce her to him. He merely said, "Do you want to marry him?"

"Papa!" Meti exclaimed. "I don't even know this man. I have never seen any of these people before. I don't want to marry someone I don't know."

"What do you want to do, marry a white man?" Wusik demanded angrily.

Missionary nurse Virginia Stimer came out of the nursing school where Meti had worked that day. "Why are you still here, Meti?"

Papa says one of these men wants to marry me and has come to take me to his village. I don't know any of these people, and I don't want to marry someone I don't know," Meti explained.

Virginia was chagrined, but she knew there was nothing she could do to help the girl.

Meti is Wusik and Nua's oldest child. She entered the world in a hut made of woven cane and thatched with *kunai*. The floor was packed earth. Her home was simple and stark, but she was surrounded by breathtaking tropical beauty. The towering mountains shrouded in white mist every morning were covered with flowers of every variety. Bananas, pineapples, pumpkins, papaya, oranges, and other fruits and vegetables supplemented her basic diet of *kaukau*, a variety of sweet potato.

When she was seven years old, her papa enrolled her in the Nazarene Community School in Kudjip. Wusik understood the value of schooling and wanted his children to be educated. Further, sending his children to school would enhance his standing in his community and increase his chances of becoming the head man in his village.

In the absence of a road, Meti walked the rocky paths from her home in Kawi to Kudjip. During the rainy season she arrived at school with mud-caked feet and muck splashed on her clothing. Meti rose before daybreak and ate a *kaukau*, which she took from the ashes of the fire that kept her warm overnight. When the sun came up she placed a second *kaukau* in her *bilum* to be eaten cold for lunch. The walk in the chilly morning air sharpened Meti's appetite, and long before she reached school she was hungry again. To allay her hunger she picked up seeds along the path and ate them. After the long walk to school, little Meti was almost too tired to concentrate and learn.

"The first four years of school, since there were few roads, there weren't many cars," Meti remembers. "Then a main road was built, and cars and trucks were often seen. We would catch rides with truck drivers and pay for the rides with *kaukau.* We weren't so tired when we got to school."

Meti was a bright child who enjoyed learning her lessons from her New Guinea teachers. She learned to speak English. She especially enjoyed Bible and religion classes taught by the missionaries.

One day, when she was in the sixth grade, the missionary gave an opportunity for the children to give their lives to Christ. Meti accepted that invitation. Even though Meti's natural disposition was sunny, she had even more joy when she began her life with Christ. Her shining brown eyes and friendly smile attracted people to her. They soon learned that she possessed intelligence and maturity unusual for one her age.

Meti finished her education by completing the sixth grade at the little Nazarene school. After that she stayed at home and learned to be a proper PNG wife. One didn't need a lot of book knowledge to tend gardens and raise pigs. That was the only life a girl could look forward to as a Western Highlands woman.

In spite of her limited opportunities, God had plans for Meti. She became a member of the Church of the Nazarene in her village.

Even though she was only eleven years old, the people at church recognized that she already knew a lot about God and the Bible. The church board appointed her to be a Sunday school teacher to the youngest children.

"This work was new to me, but I knew that before I was born God had a plan for my life," Meti said. She tried to remember the teaching methods her teachers had used at the community school. She had no trouble remembering the missionaries' Bible stories. They had come to life for her. She felt she personally knew the characters in the stories. And Jesus was as real to her as was her papa.

Meti fulfilled her duties as a Sunday school teacher so admirably that before long she was appointed church board secretary. She would keep records of the meetings and write letters that needed to be written. This was a lot of responsibility for one in her early teens, but she was the best-educated person in the church. She was one of the few people in her village who could read and write. Meti could speak and write both Pidgin and standard English. Most of the other villagers spoke only *tok ples*, their local tribal language. The young girl was conscientious and faithful in her church work, and new opportunities opened to her.

One life-changing day, Meti's pastor received a letter from a missionary who worked at the hospital on the mission compound. She was so busy at the hospital that she needed someone to work in her home. Did the pastor know of someone he could recommend?

The pastor immediately thought of Meti. She was quick to learn and had an insatiable desire to know more. She was conscientious and dependable. She would make a good *haus meri* for the missionary.

"The missionary's name was Ellen Syvret," related Meti. "She was from England. I knew nothing about how the missionaries lived. I had to learn many new skills. In my village home, meals were cooked over a cookfire started with bamboo sticks and dried grass. I was afraid to turn on the propane-gas stove in Ellen's kitchen. I had never talked on the telephone. The thought of using anything electric scared me since we didn't have electricity in the village. The missionary was kind and patient. I soon learned to do my work so she was pleased with it."

Meti learned so well that she was asked to clean the rooms at the nursing school at the mission station. Her life was good. In a country of 95-percent unemployment, she had paying jobs. She was learning new skills every day. God was working out his purpose in this talented girl's life.

Then came the day her life drastically changed. She had finished her work at the nursing school at two o'clock in the afternoon on December 31. When she left the building she noticed a large group of men gathered back of the hospital. Her papa was among them, and she went to him to find out why the crowd had gathered. He told her that one of the men had paid a bride price for her and that he and his family had come to take her to his home.

It soon became apparent that nothing she could say would reverse Wusik's decision. A high bride price had been agreed upon. Her new husband's family would be insulted if Wusik did not keep his part of the bargain. Wusik himself would be humiliated, and as a head man he would lose respect in his own tribe.

Meti wildly thought of running away and taking refuge at the mission station. Reason told her that it would be futile. Her father, or men from her husband's village, would bring her back and beat her, or worse. She asked permission to say goodbye to the missionaries. It was denied.

As a temporary compromise, Wusik told her she could return home for the present. "I was trapped, with no friend to help me," Meti said. "The laws and customs of our village must be kept. That night I secretly went to my missionary friends' homes and told them why I wouldn't see them again. We all cried together."

The next night, Friday, the men in the village made a big fire. There was singing and dancing, and everyone feasted on pig. All the men and young people in the village and among Meti's relatives came to celebrate the marriage.

Meti still had not been told which man was her husband. She didn't know anything about him or even what he looked like. She didn't know if he was a Christian. She didn't know his name. She was too angry and sad to ask.

On Saturday the men from her husband's village brought the bride price to Wusik. One thousand *kina* (in American money a little more than $300), thirty pigs, and a cassowary (the national bird of PNG) changed hands. Meti's intelligence, education, and dependability merited a substantial bride price. Meti would soon learn another reason for her high price tag.

"Early Sunday morning Virginia came to my house to bring a gift. It was hard for us to think we would not see each other again. We cried over my situation. I was so sad I could not bear to watch my friend walk out of the village, up the muddy road to the mission station," Meti remembered.

Later that day the men from her husband's tribe came to take Meti to her new home. Since her father was financially comfortable, Meti had more possessions than most brides. The men crammed her mattress, a radio, her clothing, everything that was hers, into a car. They surrounded her so she could not escape and forced her into the vehicle. Wusik watched and consented to everything that happened.

Meti was distressed that her mother, Nua, made no protest to any of this. But it would not have occurred to her to do so. Everything transpired according to Papua New Guinea custom. A mother might make a show of defending her daughter, even hiding her from her captives. But it is only a game played as part of the wedding celebration. The mother may actually cooperate with the abductors. Her only part in the wedding is to wail loudly at the loss of her daughter. New Guinea brides were not expected to feel happy about being married.

Meti's spirits sank at the sight of her new home. It was a small, dilapidated hut that needed to be replaced. There were none of the amenities she had enjoyed as the daughter of a village head man. The house was filled with people she did not know. She was quiet and sullen while everyone else celebrated the marriage she did not want.

Late in the afternoon someone said, "That man over there is your husband. You must fix him something to eat." It was the first time she had known which man she had married. His name was Tol. With sadness she discovered that he was not a Christian.

At bedtime the mattress she had enjoyed at her old home was nowhere to be seen. Exhausted, she lay down on the dirt floor and welcomed sleep. In the middle of the night she awoke, confused, not knowing where she was. The hard ground and her aching muscles reminded her of the events of the day. "Oh, God," she prayed in anguish. "Why did you send me to people I don't know?"

There was no answer. It seemed that even God had betrayed her.

On Sunday she wanted to attend her beloved church. "You can go to church with my parents," Tol insisted. Meti's new in-laws attended a church that was much different from the Church of the Nazarene. Meti, not knowing their beliefs or ways of worship, and not knowing anyone who attended there, at first refused to go with them. However, she soon realized that if she were to go to church at all, it would be at her mother- and father-in-law's church. She began attending with them.

When she went to the market to sell garden produce or buy supplies, Tol strictly admonished her to transact her business and return home immediately. She was not to linger to visit with her friends.

It was not long before Meti discovered the reason her father had received an unusually high bride price for her. Tol was known as a *stilman* (robber). He sold the missing mattress, clothing, her prized radio, and every other comfort she had brought from home. Not willing to work, stealing was the only way he could support his *buai* and *spak* habits and his sinful lifestyle.

Before his marriage he had refused to take responsibility as a man. His time was spent with friends who had a similar value system. Meti learned that the tribal leaders had become concerned about Tol's irresponsible actions and his failure to work and accumulate a bride price so he could marry. Unmarried men are not respected in PNG. Because they have no wives to work their gardens and care for pigs, they cannot accumulate wealth. Eventually they may become dependent upon the tribe for their livelihood.

Tol's fellow tribesmen decided that each one would contribute to a bride price fund, which Tol was expected to repay. Since Tol was still unmotivated to marry, the men in his village began to look for a wife for him.

They first looked among their own tribe, but no father wanted to consign his daughter to a life with Tol. The next possibility was to find a wife in a neighboring tribe. The reluctant bridegroom's reputation was widespread, and no one was interested. With every refusal the bride price increased. Finally, Tol's family approached Wusik with an irresistible offer, and he agreed to accept the bride price.

Meti fell into a deep depression. Because she could no longer attend her church, she could not teach her beloved *pikinini* or continue as church board secretary. She could not bring herself to be a proper wife to her husband. Physical abuse blighted her days. Fearful of being beaten if she refused to cooperate with him, she found other ways to express her anger.

One way she indulged her passive resistance was in doing his laundry. "I wouldn't do it at all until he insisted on it. When I couldn't put it off any longer, I would take his clothes to the river and wash them, but I wouldn't use soap." Her twinkling eyes and triumphant smile betrayed that she still felt satisfaction for her payback for his abuse. "He never knew what I had done."

"I lost my work at the church, and much sadness came into my life," Meti related. "I thought about killing myself. I did not want to be his wife. I cried a lot."

At one point Meti learned that Wusik was again living with Sarah. She returned to her own mother's home, thinking Nua would allow her to stay there. When Wusik heard about it, he came to Nua's house and insisted that his daughter go back to her husband. "It would ruin my reputation as a village head man if you return to my home," he said. He gave her sixty *kina* and a pig and sent her back to Tol.

By this time, Meti had discovered that she was expecting her first child. Life was no longer worth living, and she chose the method of suicide most common among PNG women. She drank bleach and ate poison plants.

"But God did not want my life to end," Meti said. "He still had plans for my life." By the time her friends found her, welts covered her body, and she was too weak to walk. They carried her to the emergency room at the Nazarene hospital in Kudjip. Her stomach was emptied of the poisons, and she was released to her friends.

"I gave birth to my first baby, a girl. I named her Edna. Before long I had another child, a boy. His name is Jeremiah."

Life continued in the same repressive and depressive pattern. Tol persisted in his physical and emotional abuse. Troubles mounted.

Tol's brothers and the other tribesmen had kept a record of the amount Tol owed them for the bride price they had collected. In normal circumstances a couple works together to pay off this debt. Tol was still living a playboy lifestyle and had no intention of repaying his brothers and friends. They began to pressure Meti for payment instead. She worked harder than ever to make small payments on the bride price that had been the beginning of her despair.

Meti appealed to her father for help. "You got a big bride price for me," she said. "It's very hard for me to work enough to pay this debt. I need your help." But it was as though Wusik were deaf.

Tol's grandfather recognized her plight. Although he was too old and weak to work in the garden, he took care of the children while Meti worked even longer hours to earn money to eliminate the debt.

In 1994, neighboring tribes began a war in Kudjip. All the people living there escaped to other villages. Meti and her family fled to Kawi, the place she called home. "While we were there I gave birth to another baby boy, Lesily. I took my children and went back to the Nazarene church. I was still sad, and I talked to my pastor and the members of the church board, and they began to pray for me."

The church women had a ladies' prayer meeting on Thursday morning at ten o'clock. Meti asked Tol's permission to attend. He reluctantly said she could go if her day's work was done before she left home. Meti had to rise very early in order to get food for the day, cultivate the garden, take care of the pig, and do her housework. Only then could she go to pray and fellowship with her church friends.

On one occasion Meti stood in front of the group and shared with them about her life with Tol and how depressed she was. She asked for their prayers. The women began to help Meti bear her burden by praying and showing their loving concern.

The congregation had grown so much that it was divided into four churches. The board members had not forgotten that Meti was a talented young woman. They again appointed her to teach a Sunday school class. She was interested in world mission and became president of the Nazarene Missions International (NMI) chapter in her church.

Meti continued with her heavy workload. She could not pray in her house, but while she worked in the garden she fired volleys of petitions to heaven for her husband. She asked God to work in his *bel* and bring him to repentance and salvation. When the home atmosphere was too uncomfortable, she fled the house to pray on the pretext of caring for the pig. Sometimes it seemed the heavens were closed to her. Tol continued his abuse and sinful practices.

In all this, Meti tried to live Christ in front of her husband. No matter what outrageous demands he made, or how irresponsibly he behaved, she did not berate or argue with him. She prayed that Tol would see Jesus in her life and want to know him too.

Meti prayed; the ladies prayed; her pastor prayed; the church board prayed. Since Meti was careful to meet all of Tol's demands, he allowed her and the children to attend church. He himself steadfastly refused to attend.

The time came for the church's annual district assembly and conventions. As NMI president, Meti was a delegate to both the missionary convention and the assembly. Again, the price to attend was to rise early enough to complete all her household chores before she left the house.

The church was crowded when Meti arrived, and she sat down in the last row of benches. She was paying rapt attention to convention business when, without warning, Tol entered the church, came to her, and struck her hard across the face. She was so stunned it took her a moment to comprehend what had happened and who had committed the deed. Reeling with pain, surprise, and embarrassment, Meti walked out of the church. "Why did he hit me?" she grieved. "I did all my work before I left home. He has beaten me many times at home, but he has never before attacked me in a public place."

Two ladies left the church and found Meti in the churchyard. They comforted and prayed for her. The district missionary president left the convention and brought Meti back into the church. Leading her to the front, the president explained what had happened. Convention proceedings were suspended while the entire delegation went to prayer for Meti and Tol.

When Wusik heard of Tol's offense, he was incensed. "Why did you beat her in front of all those people?" he demanded of his son-in-law. He told Meti she should divorce Tol. Before making that decision, Meti consulted with her pastor and the spiritually mature members of the church. Several issues were considered. In PNG the children belong to their father. A divorce would mean that Tol would rear the children in his own sinful way of life, if he reared them at all. Meti was young. If she divorced Tol, another man could pay a bride price for her and repeat Tol's abuse and neglect. It seemed best to the soldiers of the faith that Meti should not seek a divorce but continue to be Tol's wife and trust God for his salvation.

Word got back to Tol's village that Wusik was encouraging Meti to divorce him. The tribal leaders also knew that Tol would have custody of the children. Because he persisted in being irresponsible, they knew that the children would have to be cared for by the tribe. Not wanting this to happen, the tribal leaders encouraged him to make peace with Meti and keep the marriage intact. God was working for both Meti and her husband.

As part of the reconciliation, Tol decided he would attend church. Occasionally he would come and sit in the back of the sanctuary. Meti, the church board members, and the pastor doubled their prayer efforts. Soon Tol was in church every Sunday. There he learned that he was a sinner and doomed to destruction if he did not repent and begin to follow God. He learned about Christ's love for him and death on the cross on Tol's behalf.

One Sunday morning, as the pastor preached, God's Spirit spoke to Tol. When the invitation was given, he walked to the front, knelt at the altar, and confessed his sin to God. He asked Christ to come into his life and change him.

Everyone present knew a radical change had taken place when Tol stood. "I have not been a good man," he admitted. "I have mistreated my family. I took my wife's clothing and other belongings and sold them to buy *buai* and *spak.*" He electrified the congregation when he turned to Meti and asked her to forgive him for the abuse he had heaped on her. He then asked his children if they would forgive him.

All of this could only have been a miracle from God. It is unheard of in PNG culture for a man to ask his wife to forgive him. Of course, Meti freely forgave Tol, and their children followed her example. Tol walked out of the church a changed man.

From that time on Tol gave evidence of the transformation God had completed in his heart. He was baptized, and the pastor and church members encouraged him as he matured in the Christian faith. He was a diligent Bible student, and the church board appointed him as a Sunday school teacher.

Tol's conversion has changed Meti's life. "Now we are of one heart and serving God together in the church," she said, smiling. "God is blessing us spiritually and in other ways. I work at the mission station every day. While I work, Tol works in the garden and takes care of the chickens and pigs. When I get home from work, he has the evening meal ready for me. It is very unusual for a PNG husband to do this."

In fact, Tol challenges the ways of his culture when he does these things. These tasks are considered women's work, and self-respecting husbands leave this work to their wives. Tol demonstrates his Christian maturity and humble attitude when he takes care of these duties. He also adds to family income by taking labor jobs when they are available.

"Now, for the first time, we have chickens, a dog, a cat, rabbits, and pigs. We have recently had electricity put in our house for the first time. The bride price is almost completely paid. Our children are in school, in first and second places. Last year our daughter won a prize in eighth grade at the girls' high school. This year she is in the ninth grade. God has blessed all this work in my life, and he changed my life completely."

Meti rises every morning at three o'clock to pray. A little later Tol and the children rise, and the five of them start the day by praying together.

"When I was at the district assembly in the year 2003, Dr. Jim Radcliffe asked me to come to the hospital station to teach Pidgin to a new missionary, Dr. Becky Morsch. I taught her and worked inside her house too. Other new missionaries came later, and I taught them to speak Pidgin and worked as *haus meri* in their homes. In August 2004, God put a call in my heart and reminded me of the Bible verse James 1:27: 'Religion that God our Father accepts as pure and faultless is this: to look after orphans and widows in their distress and to keep oneself from being polluted by the world.' God gave me a ministry to orphans and widows. I prayed a lot about it. In the month of October I thought of Mark 16:15: 'Go into all the world and preach the gospel to all creation.' This verse strengthened me because the NMI slogan was *Pray, Give, Go.* Even though I am not able to go to another country to do God's work, I have a big hunger to do the work he has given me. I am happy, and I say thank you to Papa God for this call he put in my heart for all the children whose mamas and papas have died, and old women whose husbands have died, and all the old men whose wives have died, and the men and women who have HIV. I see this work is very big.

"I explained my call to my husband and my sister, who is a Christian. We three are in true unity in this ministry. They helped me, and I started the work on the sixth of October, 2004. My husband chopped firewood, and we collected cooking oil, soap, salt, clothes, and garden foods and took them to the houses of the needy. We went and had fellowship and a worship service. I prayed with them and afterward gave clothing and food to them. This is truly important work in our church. I pray and give, and I see lots of people who are sad and have problems, and I work with all these *pikinini* and *man* and *meri* (children and men and women). 'That is why I am suffering as I am. Yet this is no cause for shame, because I know whom I have believed, and am convinced that he is able to guard what I have entrusted to him until that day' (2 Timothy 1:12)."

God stood at Meti's side through the years of abuse and depression, and he delivered her from the lion's mouth. After years of hardship, she and Tol are prospering financially. Their three children are clean, well dressed, do well in school, and are polite and friendly. Meti and Tol have become the hands of Christ, working together to relieve suffering and spiritual bondage in their village of Kawi and in Pokorumb, a neighboring village. They are obeying Christ's call to go to Judea and to Samaria to rescue others from the lion's mouth.

4. The Lion Is Not Rampant

"Finally, be strong in the Lord and in his mighty power. For our struggle is not against flesh and blood, but against the rulers, against the authorities, against the powers of this dark world, and against the spiritual forces of evil in the heavenly realms."
—*Ephesians 6:10, 12*

Was the man who accosted Mike on the dark road truly Satan? Was he the witch doctor who lived on the mountaintop above Aura? Was he one of Satan's demons? What of the spirits in and around the house? The old woman of superhuman strength?

In the religious tradition of the Western world, there has been little concern about spiritual warfare as Mike experienced it. In fact, most Christians relegate it to the trash bin of superstition and hysteria. We are much more familiar with the kind of spiritual warfare Sarah and Meti fought. As their stories show, Satan's ways of waging spiritual battle are many and of endless variety.

The chief weapon used by all three of these heroes was prayer. Mike took part in an all-night prayer meeting before his encounter. During the day, he had conversation with God in which God began to prepare him for the battle. During Satan's attack, he and George maintained a prayer vigil. Sarah and the missionaries prayed for several months before she received direction concerning her future. Meti, her pastor, and other mature Christians prayed fervently and specifically that God would save Tol. God's Word tells us that "the prayer of a righteous person is powerful and effective" (James 5:16b).

Another factor in the lives of these victorious Christians was their utter abandonment to the will of God.

Mike prayed, "I'm happy to do what you want, but I'm so inadequate. Give me wisdom and strength to face whatever is coming."

Sarah said, "I will keep on working for God no matter what Wusik does." She spoke of humbling herself before the Lord.

In spite of years of abuse and depression, Meti did not lose her faith in God or her zeal for his work. She thanks God for the call he placed on her heart. Her entire life is dedicated to serving God in any way he asks.

Though Satan seems to reveal himself most commonly in countries that do not have a predominantly Christian heritage, demonic forces are occasionally reported in places like the United States. Hollywood studios make millions of dollars feeding the insatiable hunger of those fascinated with the subject. It is common to hear mediums on the airwaves mention their spirit guides, God, Jesus, and the Holy Spirit in the same sentence. As Western culture becomes increasingly focused on the occult, Christians here may find themselves face to face with demonic spirits.

Mike spoke truth when he said to his adversary, "You will be defeated." His authority was Revelation 20:10: "And the devil, who deceived them, was thrown into the lake of burning sulfur, where the beast and the false prophet had been thrown. They will be tormented day and night for ever and ever."

The apostle Paul wrote to the church in Ephesus, "Put on the full armor of God, so that you can take your stand against the devil's schemes (Ephesians 6:11). He then lists the component parts of the armor: "truth, righteousness, the gospel of peace, faith, salvation, and the word of God" (vv. 14–17).

We can rest in the assurance that the reason Jesus came was to destroy the devil's work. The lion is not rampant. He does not run unchecked and without restraint. God is always in control. Trust him.

Photos

Meti translates as Sarah and Nua tell their stories to Avonlea. Left to right: Meti (with her back to the camera), Avonlea, Sarah, Nua.

The clouds filling the valley in front of Earl and Avonlea's PNG home.

A bush church and congregation.

The interior of a bush church. The fruit and vegetables in the front are the pastor's salary for the week.

Worshipers in a bush church.

Charts like the ones Wanda and Sarah used to teach Bible stories and Scripture are still used in bush churches. Here the pastor's wife tells the story of Jesus, the Good Watchman of the sheep.

One of several people baptized on the day their new church was dedicated.

A marketplace.

It took a driver with steady hands and nerves to get this vehicle safely across the bridge.

Women with bilums hanging from their heads taking produce to market.

Sidney and Wanda Knox Memorial Church on the Kudjip station.

Nua.

Meti, Lesily, and Edna.

Wusik and a grandson.

Avonlea and Earl being honored by one of the bush churches. Earl built a pulpit for the church as an Easter surprise for the pastor.

Glossary

Apinun: afternoon. "Apinun!" is the greeting one gives from noon until after dark.

Bel: As in belly. The seat of affections, emotions, and thought.

Belhat: Hot belly. Angry.

Bikpela: Literally, big fellow. A large, great, well-known, famous, important person. When it is capitalized, it refers to God the Father, addressed as Papa God.

Bilum: A net bag made of string or yarn. Used by both men and women to carry loads. Mothers carry their babies in them, or and hang them in the nearest tree, where the baby sleeps while they work their gardens.

Buai: A recreational drug made from betel nuts and lime.

Haus: A house or hut.

Kago: English: cargo. Supplies, baggage.

Kapa: Sheet metal, galvanized roofing, tin.

Kaukau: A sweet potato. The staple diet in the Highlands.

Kina: The base monetary unit. In past years it was a shell used as a medium of exchange. Now they are coins. One kina is worth about thirty-three cents in U.S. currency.

Kunai: Grass.

Man: Pronounced mahn. A male human or animal.

Meri: A female human or animal. A *haus meri* is one who is hired to do housework. A *gaden meri* is hired to tend vegetable and flower gardens.

Misa: The Roman Catholic celebration of the Eucharist (Mass).

Nem: Name.

Pikinini: An infant, child, son, or daughter. A son is a *pikinini man*; a daughter is a *pikinini meri*. No matter the age, a son or daughter is always the parent's pikinini. It is not a term of derision.

PNG: Papua New Guinea.

Planti: A great quantity. Plenty, much, many.

Spak: An alcoholic beverage. To get or be drunk.

Stilman: A robber or thief.

Tok Ples: The language spoken locally. One's native language. There are many tribal variations.

Made in the USA
Coppell, TX
08 September 2021

61967293R00033